W9-CHS-775

HISTORY JUST BEFORE YOU WERE BORN

HURRICANE KATRINA

BY FLETCHER C. FINCH

Gareth Stevens
PUBLISHING

Please visit our website, www.garethstevens.com. For a free color catalog of all our high-quality books, call toll free 1-800-542-2595 or fax 1-877-542-2596.

Cataloging-in-Publication Data

Names: Finch, Fletcher C.
Title: Hurricane Katrina / Fletcher C. Finch.
Description: New York : Gareth Stevens Publishing, 2019. | Series: History just before you were born | Includes glossary and index.
Identifiers: LCCN ISBN 9781538231364 (pbk.) | ISBN 9781538230299 (library bound) | ISBN 9781538233160 (6 pack)
Subjects: LCSH: Hurricane Katrina, 2005--Juvenile literature. | Hurricanes--Louisiana--New Orleans--Juvenile literature. | Disasters--Louisiana--New Orleans--Juvenile literature. | Floods--Louisiana--New Orleans--Juvenile literature. | Disaster relief--Louisiana--New Orleans--Juvenile literature.
Classification: LCC HV636 2005.N4 F56 2019 | DDC 976.3'35064--dc23

First Edition

Published in 2019 by
Gareth Stevens Publishing
111 East 14th Street, Suite 349
New York, NY 10003

Designer: Sarah Liddell
Editor: Therese Shea

Photo credits: Cover, pp. 1, 11, 13 (top) Helifilms Australia/Contributor/Getty Images News/Getty Images; newspaper text background used throughout EddieCloud/Shutterstock.com; newspaper shape used throughout AVS-Images/Shutterstock.com; newspaper texture used throughout Here/Shutterstock.com; halftone texture used throughout xpixel/Shutterstock.com; pp. 5, 17, 23 Mario Tama/Staff/Getty Images News/Getty Images; p. 7 Titov Anton/Wikimedia Commons; p. 9 UniversalImagesGroup/Contributor/Universal Images Group/Getty Images; pp. 13 (bottom), 19 (bottom) Bloomberg/Contributor/Bloomberg/Getty Images; pp. 14, 16 BotMultichillT/Wikimedia Commons; p. 15 New York Daily News Archive/Contributor/New York Daily News/Getty Images; p. 19 (top) Melanie Stetson Freeman/Contributor/Christian Science Monitor/Getty Images; p. 21 Win McNamee/Staff/Getty Images News/Getty Images; p. 25 Benjamin Lowy/Contributor/Getty Images News/Getty Images; p. 27 Chris Graythen/Stringer/Getty Images News/Getty Images.

Printed in the United States of America

CPSIA compliance information: Batch #CW19CS: For further information contact Gareth Stevens, New York, New York at 1-800-542-2595.

CONTENTS

A NATIONAL DISASTER 4

THE GROWING STORM 6

A CITY IN DANGER 8

WIND, RAIN, AND STORM SURGES 10

UNPREPARED 12

SHELTERING IN THE SUPERDOME 14

TRAPPED ON ROOFTOPS 16

DISORDER AND VIOLENCE 18

FEMA'S RESPONSE 20

THE WORLD WATCHES 22

THE LONG ROAD 24

LASTING DAMAGE 26

KATRINA'S LEGACY 28

GLOSSARY 30

FOR MORE INFORMATION 31

INDEX 32

Words in the glossary appear in **bold** type
the first time they are used in the text.

A NATIONAL DISASTER

Hurricane Katrina was one of the deadliest and most destructive disasters in US history. It affected an area of about 90,000 square miles (233,100 sq km). The strength of the hurricane was only one of the reasons for the deaths and damage that occurred. The landscape of the area, outdated flood protection, bad planning, and poor choices contributed to the **devastation**.

Around the country and the world, people were shocked by what they saw when Hurricane Katrina hit the Gulf Coast in August 2005. Towns and cities—most notably New Orleans, Louisiana—were badly damaged, and as many as 1,800 people died during and after the storm. Those who lived through it experienced loss, violence, and disorder. Rebuilding took years, and the areas affected will never be the same.

MORE TO THE STORY

More major hurricanes from the Atlantic Ocean struck the United States in 2005 than in any past hurricane season. Areas of Mexico and the Caribbean were also hit by hurricanes that year.

Hurricanes aren't new to the Gulf Coast of the United States. In 1900, a hurricane hit the city of Galveston, Texas. That storm killed more than 6,000 people. A 1915 hurricane traveling through New Orleans killed at least 275 people. In 1965, Hurricane Betsy destroyed towns on the Louisiana coast. This storm didn't hit New Orleans directly, but caused flooding when levees, or structures built to hold back water, failed. Eighty-one people died.

STORM SURVIVORS IN NEW ORLEANS WALK TO HIGHER GROUND. BEHIND THEM ARE FLOODED CITY STREETS.

THE GROWING STORM

In late August 2005, weather forecasters noticed a storm forming near the Bahamas. The tropical depression, or low-pressure storm, grew stronger as it headed west. By the time it reached southern Florida on August 25, the wind was blowing about 80 miles (129 km) per hour. The storm knocked down trees and power lines. Several people died.

After crossing Florida, the storm gained energy from the warm waters of the Gulf of Mexico. On August 26, forecasters believed the storm could hit the coasts of Mississippi and Louisiana with even more power. People in some areas began to evacuate, or move to safety, and officials tried to prepare for a terrible storm. Hurricane Katrina hit the Gulf Coast on August 29.

MORE TO THE STORY

The US National Hurricane Center tracked Katrina's growth and movement with a special plane, satellites, radar systems, **buoys,** and reports from land and sea.

HURRICANE KATRINA IS SEEN FROM SPACE IN THIS **SATELLITE** PHOTOGRAPH FROM AUGUST 29, 2005.

HURRICANE FORMATION

Hurricanes begin near the equator. Warm, moist air rises from near the surface of the ocean, creating an area of low pressure. Air rushes in to this space and becomes warm and moist, too. It rises, leaving space for more air. The rising air forms clouds that start to swirl and creates wind. A storm strengthens as warm, moist air continues to fuel it. If the sustained winds are 74 miles (119 km) per hour or faster, the storm is called a hurricane.

A CITY IN DANGER

The danger of hurricanes wasn't foreign to New Orleans or its residents. The city traces its history to 1718, when French colonists settled near a curve in the Mississippi River close to the Gulf of Mexico. The site was hit by floods and hurricanes even from its early years, but was still an important trading post under French, then Spanish, and finally American control.

By 2005, levees and floodwalls provided the city some protection from floods, but many of these were outdated or poorly made. Moreover, global **climate change** has caused **sea levels** to rise and parts of New Orleans are lower than sea level. On August 27, Mayor Ray Nagin suggested people leave New Orleans. The next day, he ordered a **mandatory** evacuation. For thousands, that wasn't enough time before the storm struck.

MORE TO THE STORY

Flooding is dangerous. People can drown or be swept away, even in just a few inches of water. Floodwaters can also carry chemicals or bacteria from buildings and sewers the water has flowed through.

CHANGING THE LANDSCAPE

Over the years, many natural **wetlands** around New Orleans were drained for people's health and to allow new construction. This caused the ground in low areas to sink even further. Canals built for shipping allowed salt water to flow into existing wetlands, killing trees there that had provided natural protection from storms. Soil near the canals and river eroded. Small islands that protected the mainland from storms washed away. Seawater sometimes flooded canals during storms, too.

THIS SATELLITE PHOTO SHOWS NEW ORLEANS, WITH LAKE PONTCHARTRAIN AT THE TOP OF THE PHOTO AND THE MISSISSIPPI RIVER NEAR THE CENTER. LAKE PONTCHARTRAIN IS AN ESTUARY, A PLACE WHERE FRESHWATER FROM A RIVER MIXES WITH SALTY OCEAN WATER.

WIND, RAIN, AND STORM SURGES

When Hurricane Katrina hit the coast of southeastern Louisiana, it had winds over 140 miles (225 km) per hour. The wind tore at buildings, knocked down trees, and whipped boats around. Katrina also brought nearly 15 inches (38 cm) of rain to parts of the state.

Some of the most damaging elements of Katrina were storm surges. These are rises in sea levels caused by strong winds and the higher atmospheric pressure at the edge of the hurricane. Powerful surges hit the coasts of Louisiana, Mississippi, and Alabama. Places such as Gulfport and Biloxi, Mississippi, experienced flooding more than 25 feet (7.6 m) above normal tide levels. But New Orleans faced the severest devastation because many of its levees and floodwalls failed. Water poured into the city.

MORE TO THE STORY

Though Alabama wasn't as devastated by Katrina as Mississippi and Louisiana, the hurricane caused terrible damage in 22 counties along the coast and killed two people.

THIS BUILDING IN BILOXI, MISSISSIPPI, COLLAPSED WHEN
KATRINA HIT. STORM SURGES DESTROYED HOMES, ROADS,
BRIDGES, AND BUSINESSES. MORE THAN 200 PEOPLE IN
MISSISSIPPI DIED.

MISSISSIPPI DAMAGE

While much of the hurricane damage that occurred in New Orleans was the
result of levee failures, the damage in Mississippi came from the strength
of the hurricane itself. Parts of the state experienced winds measuring near
200 miles (322 km) an hour. More than 100,000 people were left homeless
after the hurricane caused at least $25 billion in damage. The devastation
spanned the Mississippi coast into Alabama but was also felt far inland.

UNPREPARED

Previous studies had shown the danger a major hurricane could bring to New Orleans, but officials had failed to prepare for a storm the strength of Katrina. The levee system was aging and attempts to strengthen it were underfunded.

During the storm, city, state, and federal officials all needed to work together, but were uncertain about their responsibilities. The mayor's evacuation order came too late, and many people couldn't leave. About 120,000 people in New Orleans didn't have cars. The city's disaster plan stated that buses should be used for evacuation, but flooding cut off many routes and even flooded the buses themselves. The city bused some people to emergency shelters, but there were many more people than expected. Thousands were still in the city, and they were in danger.

MORE TO THE STORY

The design of the levees in New Orleans didn't account for the soft soil in the area. When the water came, the soil holding some walls in place washed away. In other areas, the water flowed over the levees.

PEOPLE AT RISK

Residents who were homeless, elderly, sick, disabled, or poor were at the most risk during Hurricane Katrina. Many weren't able to evacuate by themselves, and there wasn't an organized system to help them. Medical facilities flooded, lost power, and ran low on supplies. At St. Rita's Nursing Home in St. Bernard **Parish**, 35 patients drowned. Patients died in other hospitals and nursing homes after the storm hit as well.

BROKEN LEVEE

AS LEVEES AND FLOODWALLS WERE OVERWHELMED, WATER FLOODED INTO NEW ORLEANS. SOME SPOTS WERE UNDER MORE THAN 10 FEET (3 M) OF WATER.

13

SHELTERING IN THE SUPERDOME

Tens of thousands of people were unable to evacuate New Orleans. Many headed to "shelters of last resort," including the Superdome. The Superdome was built for sports events, not to house people, but more than 20,000 people were trapped there for up to 6 days.

SUPERDOME AFTER HURRICANE KATRINA

The hurricane damaged the roof, letting water leak in. The building lost electricity and relied on a **generator** to provide some power. It had no air conditioning, so temperatures rose into the high 80s. Stored food began to rot. There were no showers, and all toilets stopped working. Food and water were in short supply, and medical care was limited. Some people became violent, and six people died of various causes.

MORE TO THE STORY

After months of construction following the hurricane, the Superdome reopened in September 2006. Its restoration was seen as a symbol of rebirth for New Orleans.

LIGHT SHINES THROUGH HOLES IN THE ROOF OF THE
SUPERDOME. PEOPLE WERE TRAPPED THERE FOR DAYS,
UNABLE TO MAKE CALLS OR HEAR NEWS FROM THE
OUTSIDE WORLD.

RUMORS AND EXAGGERATIONS

During and after the hurricane, stories of murders, gangs, and gunfire
in the Superdome spread. While there was some violence, many of the
rumors were untrue. People trapped inside wanted information about what
was going on and false stories spread quickly. National news outlets shared
some tales. New Orleans mayor Ray Nagin and police superintendent Eddie
Compass both made statements about armed gangs that later proved to
be untrue.

TRAPPED ON ROOFTOPS

About 80 percent of New Orleans flooded. As the water rose, people who were trapped in homes or other buildings tried to get above the water. Many worked their way up to attics and broke through the roof. Some couldn't escape the flood and drowned in their homes or were lost in the rushing water.

The Louisiana Department of Wildlife and Fisheries had prepared staff and boats before the storm hit. They began to search for survivors when the winds calmed down. The US Coast Guard flew helicopters in to pick up trapped residents. Police and emergency agencies joined the effort. Citizens with fishing boats also worked to save people. Still, with tens of thousands to save, the rescues took days.

MORE TO THE STORY

News reports that people were shooting at rescue helicopters were shared around the world. Officials later said some gunfire was from people trying to attract rescuers.

THE CAJUN NAVY

Ordinary citizens used their own boats to save around 10,000 people. Hundreds of **volunteers** gathered in Lafayette, Louisiana, where **Cajun** communities trace their roots to 18th-century French colonists of Canada. President George W. Bush praised these volunteers: "Fishermen used their flat-bottom boats to form the 'Cajun Navy,' and pulled women and children and the elderly out of flooded homes, and brought them to dry ground. . . . In these and countless other acts of courage, we saw the very best of America."

RESCUERS IN A BOAT HELP PEOPLE TRAPPED ON THE ROOF OF THE DR. MARTIN LUTHER KING JR. CHARTER SCHOOL FOR SCIENCE AND TECHNOLOGY IN NEW ORLEANS.

DISORDER AND VIOLENCE

The survivors of Hurricane Katrina needed food, water, and other essentials. Some got what they needed from stores. Others took advantage of the destruction and confusion to steal valuables from homes and businesses. This made rescue efforts harder. New Orleans police—who had been searching for survivors and helping people leave—were told to focus on keeping order.

Fear of theft led some people to keep watch over their homes and stores with weapons. Violent confrontations erupted in the city. Black residents reported unfair treatment by law enforcement officials. There were also accusations of racially motivated violence by armed citizens. Many people in New Orleans and the Gulf Coast felt abandoned or betrayed by the government.

MORE TO THE STORY

Most New Orleans police officers provided assistance during the storm, but more than 200 left the city without permission. Superintendent Eddie Compass resigned after the storm.

A SIGN IN THE ALGIERS NEIGHBORHOOD OF NEW ORLEANS THREATENS THIEVES.

THE DANZIGER BRIDGE SHOOTINGS

On September 4, police reported gunfire at Danziger Bridge. A group of New Orleans police officers not in uniform arrived. They shot at unarmed people who were walking on the bridge. Two of the people died and others were seriously injured. The officers at first said they had been shot at and were defending themselves. Four were later convicted in the killings. Another was convicted for lying in the investigation.

FEMA'S RESPONSE

The Federal Emergency Management Agency (FEMA) coordinates the national government's response to disasters. It prepares for emergencies, **mitigates** problems, and organizes recovery programs.

After Hurricane Katrina, police officers, firefighters, and other people from agencies outside the area hit by the storm were willing to help, but FEMA didn't know how to coordinate these workers in their efforts. So, volunteers who wanted to help were delayed or their assistance was disorganized.

In some cases, FEMA did take charge, but mistakenly made things worse. FEMA staff sent away trucks with donated water. They stopped the Coast Guard from bringing in fuel that would have been useful and cut an emergency communications line. Some people waited days for help to arrive after the storm.

MORE TO THE STORY

A congressional committee investigated the response to Hurricane Katrina. It reported FEMA's staff didn't have the experience and training needed to deal with the disaster.

"HECK OF A JOB"

In a September 2 press conference, President George W. Bush praised FEMA director Michael Brown. "Brownie, you're doing a heck of a job," he said. The president's encouragement of Brown didn't cheer the many people still suffering in affected areas, though. News reporters brought attention to many issues. Local and state officials complained publicly about the slow and mismanaged federal response. Ten days later, Michael Brown resigned from his post as director.

RESIDENTS IN BILOXI, MISSISSIPPI, AND OTHER COMMUNITIES QUESTIONED FEMA'S SLOW RESPONSE.

THE WORLD WATCHES

Hurricane Katrina captured the attention of the world. Americans wondered how such a terrible disaster could happen in their country. Some news coverage was incorrect, but it was clear that mismanagement had made things worse.

Aaron Broussard, the president of Jefferson Parish in Louisiana, condemned the government's response on national television. "We have been abandoned by our own country," he said. "Hurricane Katrina will go down in history as one of the worst storms ever to hit an American coast, but the aftermath of Hurricane Katrina will go down as one of the worst abandonments of Americans on American soil ever in US history. . . . **Bureaucracy** has committed murder here in the greater New Orleans area and bureaucracy has to stand trial before Congress now."

MORE TO THE STORY

The Lower Ninth Ward was the hardest hit community of New Orleans. When floodwalls failed, the rushing water pushed houses off their foundations. Parts of the community were covered by up to 12 feet (3.7 m) of water for weeks.

SCENES LIKE THIS POST–HURRICANE DAMAGE WERE BROADCAST AROUND THE WORLD.

KANYE CRITICIZES THE PRESIDENT

During a live television fundraiser for hurricane relief on September 2, musician Kanye West spoke out. West criticized the slow federal response, blaming it on racism. He concluded, "George Bush doesn't care about black people." Bush denied that statement and called it the "all-time low" of his presidency. While West later said he regretted his words, his anger reflected the frustrations of many blacks in New Orleans who felt abandoned by the government.

THE LONG ROAD

With homes and communities damaged along the Gulf Coast, storm survivors needed to find help and shelter. An analysis by *USA Today* showed that about 240,000 survivors had headed to Houston, Dallas, or San Antonio in Texas, Atlanta in Georgia, or to other places within about 500 miles (805 km). Around 60,000 people went to communities more than 750 miles (1,207 km) away. In fact, hurricane survivors were reported in every US state. Some of those who left the Gulf Coast never returned.

About 452,000 people lived in New Orleans before Katrina. More than half their homes were severely damaged in the storm. In January 2006, only around 210,000 people lived in the city. However, by 2016, the population had grown to more than 390,000.

MORE TO THE STORY

Ten years after Katrina, only about 37 percent of families had returned to the Lower Ninth Ward of New Orleans.

THE CHANGING FACE OF NEW ORLEANS

The people who came to New Orleans after Katrina weren't always the same ones who had left because of the storm. In 2016, black residents made up a smaller percentage of the population than before the hurricane, while white and Hispanic residents made up a larger percentage. Many new residents came to New Orleans seeking employment in the rebuilding process and decided to stay. Some opened new businesses.

FEMA PROVIDED MORE THAN 130,000 TRAILERS AND MOBILE HOMES AS EMERGENCY HOUSING.

LASTING DAMAGE

Immediately after Hurricane Katrina, Congress approved aid packages to help storm victims and recovery programs. The shape that recovery would take wasn't clear. Some leaders questioned whether to rebuild in an area at risk from future storms.

Homeowners and governments fought insurance companies for money to fix houses. Nonprofit organizations and volunteers helped storm victims along the coast. The American Red Cross provided shelter, and Habitat for Humanity constructed new homes. The Army Corps of Engineers, who were blamed for levee failures, built new flood protection systems.

Some of the poor communication and mismanagement that had delayed rescue efforts also slowed recovery programs. New Orleans mayor Ray Nagin and others were later convicted of the crime of taking money or favors from companies in exchange for valuable rebuilding contracts.

MORE TO THE STORY

In the year after Hurricane Katrina, more than 575,500 volunteers gave their time to help recovery efforts. Millions more donated money and supplies.

A MAN WORKS TO CLEAR OUT A FRIEND'S HOUSE IN THE LAKEVIEW AREA OF NEW ORLEANS. MOLD WAS A PROBLEM IN THE RECOVERY EFFORTS. IT ROTS HOUSES AND CAUSES ILLNESSES.

SYMBOLS OF RECOVERY

Since 2005, tourism and recreation have brought visitors and money back to areas hit by Katrina. New hotels and casinos attract people to Biloxi and other parts of Mississippi's coast. In New Orleans, Mardi Gras and other festivals have drawn people back year after year. In 2016, visitors to New Orleans spent over $7 billion, and the city welcomed a record-breaking 10.45 million tourists, the largest number since 2004.

KATRINA'S LEGACY

Geography, poor preparation, and human error played a role in what happened after Hurricane Katrina hit. It was both a natural and man-made disaster. The tragedy shook people's faith in the US government and exposed serious problems in its response to an emergency.

Speaking a few weeks after the storm, Louisiana governor Kathleen Blanco said, "We all know that there were failures at every level of government: state, federal, and local. At the state level, we must take a careful look at what went wrong and make sure it never happens again."

Much of New Orleans and the Gulf Coast have rebuilt, but even those efforts were difficult. The areas affected will never be the same. People have shown **resilience**, but the lives destroyed and lost will forever haunt the region.

MORE TO THE STORY

In the 10 years after Katrina, $14.5 billion was spent to protect the New Orleans area, including building stronger levees, pumps, and floodgates.

New Orleans is better prepared now for a hurricane than it was in 2005. However, many other areas of the country have coastal erosion and construction in low-lying areas, factors that added to the damage of Katrina. The 2017 hurricane season was the most costly for the United States since 2005. Hurricane Harvey hit the Texas Gulf Coast, Hurricane Irma struck Florida, and Hurricane Maria made landfall in Puerto Rico, causing deaths and widespread destruction.

HURRICANE KATRINA TIMELINE

AUGUST 23, 2005: THE US NATIONAL HURRICANE CENTER REPORTS A STORM IS FORMING NEAR THE BAHAMAS.

AUGUST 24: THE STORM STRENGTHENS AND IS GIVEN THE NAME KATRINA.

AUGUST 25: HURRICANE KATRINA STRIKES SOUTHERN FLORIDA, NEAR MIAMI.

AUGUST 26: THE GOVERNOR OF LOUISIANA DECLARES A STATE OF EMERGENCY.

AUGUST 27: THE STORM STRENGTHENS AS IT CROSSES THE GULF OF MEXICO. THE GOVERNOR OF MISSISSIPPI DECLARES A STATE OF EMERGENCY.

AUGUST 28: MAYOR NAGIN ANNOUNCES THE MANDATORY EVACUATION OF NEW ORLEANS. THOUSANDS SEEK SHELTER IN THE SUPERDOME. THE GOVERNOR OF ALABAMA DECLARES A STATE OF EMERGENCY.

AUGUST 29: THE STORM REACHES THE SHORE OF LOUISIANA. LATER, IT HITS THE CITIES OF BILOXI AND GULFPORT, MISSISSIPPI.

AUGUST 30: THE STORM SYSTEM WEAKENS AND MOVES AWAY, BUT WATER CONTINUES TO SPILL INTO NEW ORLEANS.

AUGUST 31: LOUISIANA GOVERNOR KATHLEEN BLANCO ORDERS PEOPLE STILL IN NEW ORLEANS TO LEAVE.

SEPTEMBER 2: US NATIONAL GUARD TROOPS ARRIVE WITH SUPPLIES FOR PEOPLE IN THE SUPERDOME.

SEPTEMBER 4: POLICE OFFICERS SHOOT UNARMED CIVILIANS ON DANZIGER BRIDGE.

SEPTEMBER 5: THE ARMY CORPS OF ENGINEERS STARTS TO PUMP WATER OUT OF NEW ORLEANS.

OCTOBER 3: THE SEARCH FOR VICTIMS OF THE STORM ENDS.

OCTOBER 11: THE LAST OF THE FLOODWATER IS PUMPED OUT OF NEW ORLEANS.

GLOSSARY

buoy: a floating object used to guide ships, mark a place in the water, or for another purpose

bureaucracy: a system of government that has many complicated rules and ways of doing things

Cajun: a person from Louisiana whose ancestors were French colonists of Canada

climate change: long-term change in Earth's climate, caused partly by human activities such as burning oil and natural gas

devastation: damage and destruction

generator: a machine that uses moving parts to produce electrical energy

mandatory: required by a law or rule

mitigate: to make less severe, harmful, or painful

parish: a community

resilience: the ability to become strong, healthy, or successful again after something bad happens

satellite: an object that circles Earth in order to collect and send information

sea level: the average height of the sea's surface

volunteer: a person who works without being paid

wetland: land containing high levels of moisture in the soil and usually covered with water at least part of the time

FOR MORE INFORMATION

BOOKS

Burgan, Michael. *Total Devastation: The Story of Hurricane Katrina*. North Mankato, MN: Capstone Press, 2017.

Koontz, Robin. *What Was Hurricane Katrina?* New York, NY: Grosset & Dunlap, 2015.

WEBSITES

Feature Story: Voices of Katrina
www.mshistorynow.mdah.ms.gov/articles/253/voices-of-katrina
Residents of southern Mississippi share their memories of the storm and its aftermath.

Hurricane Katrina
www.knowlouisiana.org/entry/hurricane-katrina
This is an overview of Hurricane Katrina with a focus on the state of Louisiana.

The Storm: 14 Days: A Timeline
www.pbs.org/wgbh/pages/frontline/storm/etc/cron.html
This timeline features major events relating to Hurricane Katrina.

INDEX

Alabama 10, 11, 29

Army Corps of Engineers 26, 29

Bahamas 6, 29

Bush, George W. 17, 21, 23

"Cajun Navy" 17

Danziger Bridge shootings 19, 29

evacuations 6, 8, 12, 13, 14, 29

Federal Emergency Management Agency (FEMA) 20, 21, 25

flooding 5, 8, 9, 10, 12, 13, 16, 17, 29

Florida 6, 29

Gulf Coast 4, 5, 6, 18, 24, 28, 29

Gulf of Mexico 6, 8, 29

hurricane formation 7

landscape 4, 9, 12

levees 5, 8, 10, 11, 12, 13, 26, 28

Louisiana 4, 5, 6, 10, 16, 17, 22, 28, 29

Lower Ninth Ward 22, 24

Mississippi 6, 10, 11, 21, 27, 29

recovery efforts 20, 26, 27

rescue efforts 16, 17, 18, 26

storm surge 10, 11

Superdome, the 14, 15, 29

supplies 13, 14, 26, 29

Texas 5, 24, 29

theft 18, 19

US Coast Guard 16, 20

US National Hurricane Center 6, 29

violence 4, 14, 15, 18

volunteers 17, 20, 26

West, Kanye 23